Made in the USA
Columbia, SC
21 October 2023

24758014R00057